Acknowledgement

I would like to thank all of those who have touched my life in any way.

You made me who I am today!!

Sometimes it takes difficult situations to make us step out of our comfort zone and change things in our life. I count my blessings that even after all I have been through, I still have love in my heart.

I would like to thank my boss, friend, and brother from another mother (and another father). He gave me the little extra pushes and nudges to continue with this story until the end. Thank you, Tony Wilmington. It is appreciated that you, your wife, Amber, along with your entire family believed in my ability to tell my story. Y'all will always be in my thoughts, prayers and in my heart. I love each one of you!!

I never knew when God sent me to work for you that it would change my life and help me to grow and heal in such a positive way.
I am forever grateful!!

I would like to thank my friends for always inspiring me and lifting me up. I appreciate all of you for allowing me to entertain you with my stories and encouraging me. Lots of you told me over the years "you should write a book one day" so, thank you. I have the best friends in the world!!

Most of all I thank God for always lifting me up and never leaving my side, even in my darkest hours. Jesus is the reason that I can now smile and know all is well with my soul!!

Preface

This book started as a self-healing project, for me and me alone. It is the story of my journey through this life.

I know lots of people and they all know little pieces of my story, but no one knows my whole story, not even those closest to me. I was always a private person and never shared a lot about my personal life.

I decided to do this for myself to help me let go of a lot of things that I had held on to for so many years.

As I recalled, all that happened to me over the years, I decided to share my story. I did this so that someone else may gain some insight and help from what I have gone through.

With all I have endured, I became a better and stronger person each time.

My hope is that this book will perhaps give someone hope and help them to become a better, stronger person, as well.

I owe all that I am to God for saving me from all my bad decisions and all the evil people who entered my life. God has given me plenty of Angels here on this earth, which have blessed and enriched my life as well.

There is hope and happiness after abuse. We just need to learn from our mistakes and recognize the patterns that we keep repeating and make extra effort not to go back to them.

I now live an abusive free, drama
free, happy, fun filled life.

I know who I am and what I want in my life.
I am also very aware of what I DON'T want in my life.

Words to live by-
I learned all these lessons the hard way

*None of us are perfect and we just need
to be the best person that we can be.

*Wake up every day and be a better version
of yourself than you were yesterday.

*Forgive, but never forget- (forgetting
is what gets you into trouble)

*Forgive yourself and move on

*Do not look back, it is too late to change the
past, look forward to changing the future

*The only person you can change is yourself

*Some people do not want to change;
you cannot do it for them

*As bad as you want to help people,
some people do not want help

*If you try to help someone that does not want
help- they will drag you down with them

To my Beautiful
Antonie

Thank you for coming
into my life and being
such a blessing!

Love you

Donna Jean
(aka Mamacita)

Always Love from the heart!
♡

Chapter 1

Toxic Beginnings

Toxic Beginnings

I will start by saying that I have may layers, sort of like an onion.

There are many reasons that these layers have formed over the years. Some layers were to cover things up and some were to compartmentalize and survive what I had gone or was going through.

It all started on June 13, 1966. I was born into the very toxic relationship. Mom was a stay at home wife and mother. My Dad was a Marine and we were stationed in Hawaii at that time. Dad also had a part time job in a bar (from what I understand) to help provide for his growing family. Mom was an only child who had been raised by her grandparents and Dad was one of nine children.

At night, dad would often drink at the bar where he worked. Sometimes, he would run around with other women. I even heard one story that he brought a woman to our house and made my Mom drive her home.

My Dad grew up in a very abusive home and the abuse just carried over into our home. He was abusive to Mom if she did not do what she was told.

Being in the military they lived far from all the friends and the family they knew.

When I was just a toddler, we got a transfer to North Carolina.

As a little girl, my Dad was my hero. I saw him dressed in his military uniform every day and he was so handsome.

Although I never felt the wrath of my father's hand, that I can remember, but my mom and my older sister unfortunately did. I was actually so young I do not remember a whole lot, or perhaps I have blocked it out of my mind because I was too young to understand it all.

At an incredibly young age, I had bad eyesight and had to get glasses. I also wore a patch to cover my lazy eye for a short time. I remember this clearly because my sister cried for several days because I had to wear the patch and glasses.

Shortly after that, I remember us bringing my dad to the airport so he could catch a plane to go overseas to the Vietnam War. It was the beginning of my heartbreak. I was Daddy's little girl and he was gone.

Not long after he returned, mom took my sister and myself and we moved back to Louisiana. Mom moved us to Cameron, Louisiana. This is where she had grown up. My parents were getting a divorce!!

We rented a house from some people mom knew. She had lots of friends and family there and we were always doing something with them.

Mom was enjoying her new-found freedom. My sister and I were going from house to house with babysitters and family while Mom worked and enjoyed the single life.

I do not remember much about those days except I was missing my Dad, and no one seemed to care.

After some time, Mom bought a house in Lake Charles. It was a bigger town, about an hour north of the house we had rented in Cameron.

Although there were quite a few kids in our new neighborhood, most of them were older than me. So, I just played with my sister and her friends when I was allowed.

Mom worked and so she hired a babysitter, Bertha, to stay with us during the day. I absolutely loved this woman!! Bertha had a wonderful loving heart and a great sense of humor. She was always so understanding and loving. Bertha had raised 9 children of her own and now cared for other people's children. She was always so cheerful and had a great disposition. I often referred to her as "Mom" when my Mom was not around. I was a cotton top blonde haired, blue-eyed little girl with fair skin and Bertha was a colored woman. When we were in public and I would call her Mom, we would get some strange looks, to say the least.

My older sister, Cindy, was demanding more and more attention and Mom was busy trying to put her life back together. Cindy was angry about the divorce. She was so angry about having a babysitter and that Mom had to work that she just spewed anger all the time. Mom had things to do and Cindy could not be the center of attention and she let everyone know that she was not happy.

My sister's wrath eventually turned toward me. I can remember, she was always in trouble. Her temper tantrums and fits got worse and worse. One time she did not want to listen to the sitter and she just fell to the floor holding her breathe and pitching a fit. So, Bertha threw a glass of cold water on her and that really made her mad.

It was always drama and fighting around my sister. Bertha became my protector and would make sure my sister was not hitting me or pulling my hair or bossing me around.

Then, when Mom was home, she was usually busy doing other things and the abuse would escalate. I was constantly getting bossed around and if I did not do what my sister told me then she would beat me up, yell at me or pull my hair.

It really started weighing heavy on me because I loved my sister. To see her always in trouble, and always fighting or hurting me, I just did not understand. It eventually got to the point that I started wishing that whoever gave me up for adoption would come back and get me. I was not adopted, but her abuse and drama had me wishing I were. I remember crying at age 5 or 6 and hating my life. I was all alone, with no one to talk with about my terrible situation. Mom did not have time and my sister was only nice and played with me, when it was convenient for her. Otherwise, she was trying to figure out a way for revenge.

I eventually turned to food for my comfort. It was my only way to comfort myself. So, not only did I wear glasses but now I was "chubby".

Mom eventually married again and there was not much need for our sitter. That was a total devastation for me because Bertha was the only one at our house who showed me unconditional love and she was my protector from my sister's abuse.

Mom and her new husband, who we called Pop, fought a lot at first. There was never any peace in our house. Cindy also fought with them. She did not like anything about our new family.

She was still angry about the divorce and now she was even more angry about the new stepdad. It was a constant battle for our household. She was only about 8 at this, time but was a holy terror.

I did have my grandparents and they always showed unconditional love. However, they lived in the country, about an hour away and only came to visit every other week. I was always told to keep our personal life at home and not let others know of the things that happened there. After all, "What would people think?" So, I could not even talk to my grandparents about my issues at home. I did go to my grandparent's house as often as I could. Summer breaks, or any time off from school, that is where I wanted to be. My grandparent's house was a great place for me. It was so quiet, no fighting, no yelling and drama free. I would love the trips there. Just sitting on the front porch with my grandma or going to the beach to look for treasure was a treat. And all the ice cream and cookies I wanted!! (I was a chubby girl and I needed snacks.)

Mom and Pop always went out on Friday and Saturday nights. They had plans every weekend.

As it would happen, one time when Mom went out, (I will not give much detail) I was sleeping and was felt up by a close relative and he penetrated me with his finger. I could not have been more than 5 years old. I was totally mortified, terrified and embarrassed. I never told a soul. Who could I tell? I had no one that I could confide in.

Mom was busy with her new husband and my angry sister. My sister was busy creating turmoil and stating how unhappy she was. I was all alone. So, I kept it to myself and continued to pretend all was well and besides, I had my food to comfort me.

During one of our summer breaks, my Dad, who was still in the military, drove down to pick us up, and we went up to Richmond, Virginia, where he was stationed at the time. He was living the single life, so when we visited him, he had a sitter from his apartment building watch us. She watched us when he was at work. We played dress up with her and listened to lots of music. She would also put makeup on us and fix our hair.

Dad did spend some time with us and took us to an amusement park in Richmond Virginia, to tour the Washington Monument and all-around D.C. I even remember that we attended a 4th of July celebration on the military base. It was amazing, with baseball games, picnics, and fireworks. It was one of my best memories of just the three of us, Dad, Cindy, and myself. Dad did not put up with much and so no fighting around him. Although, when dad was at work my sister managed to be the "boss of me". Summer only lasted so long and back to Mom's we went to live in that toxic turmoil again.

Chapter 2

School Days

School Days

As I started school, of course the children made fun of me. I was chubby with glasses and no self-esteem. I had one part time friend who lived a couple blocks away. Every now and then I went to her house to play Barbies, but that was about it. Otherwise I would tag along with my sister and her friends when I was allowed. I just managed to get by and stay to myself. Pretending everything was ok.

When I was starting second grade, we moved just over the bridge to another town called Westlake. It was a small town and we moved on the outskirts of town in the country. Mom and Pop wanted chickens, rabbits, sheep, and horses, so here we were.

The new town was not much different from the old town because the neighbor next door was my sister's age. The kids at school would still call me things like fat and 4 eyes, then at home I was called stupid and chubby.

Sometimes my sister and her friends would let me play with them, but it was probably because Mom made them.

Although Cindy was very abusive and mean to me, she would not let anyone else be mean to me.

I remember one time we were at my cousin's house for the weekend. A boy cousin held my head under the water in the pool and my sister clobbered him. She made sure that I was protected from everyone, EXCEPT her.

I had a few new friends but mostly ones that had just moved there or ones that did not stay long. I stayed around the house a lot. Cindy now going with her friends and hardly ever home.

I learned to cook, clean and, of course, I ate. I would still go with my grandparents as much as possible for summer breaks or extended holidays from school. I loved it there!!

As we settled in a few years, I started making a few friends and would get invited to the occasional sleepover. I was still rather chubby, with glasses and awkward with no self-esteem.

When I was 10 years old, my Mom and Stepdad had a baby girl, Janet. Now she was the center of attention! There was more laundry to do and the house was a little quieter sometimes, so as not to wake the baby.

Cindy was a teenager and more interested in going places, and spending time with her friends so she was ok with this, most of the time.

There were still fights when Cindy got caught doing things she was not supposed to be doing and she would get punished. Or she wanted to take something that I had, and I did not want her to have it. My Mom and Stepdad had mostly toned down their fighting and arguing.

I was starting to do a little more with the small group of friends I had made. Life was a little peaceful for a while.

On the last day of 7th grade, as I descended the stairwell in the hallway, a boy named Evan accidentally touched my hand. He was so cute!! I was so excited that he had even touched my hand because I had been noticing him in the hallway. To tell the truth he probably did not even notice that he had touched my hand. My heart went wild, but he was a year older than me and he would be going to high school next year.

We rarely saw my Dad. When we did, he did not tell us much about his personal life. Imagine our surprise when unexpectedly, he got married to a lady from New York.

Over that summer my dad and my new stepmom came to pick us up, along with my half-sister and the two stepsisters. (Dad eventually adopted the two girls. that belonged to my new stepmom.) We all went to my paternal grandparent's house to spend a week. It was uneventful the first few days. We just played with our cousins and hung out.

One-night Dad, his wife and my grandparents went out for a while. When they came home my grandfather was drunk and in a rage. My Dad locked all of us girls along with my stepmom, in the bedroom and told us not to open the door for any reason. Then my grandfather was yelling and was beating on the bedroom door. He was wanting in and from what I gathered he wanted sex, and he did not care from who. Anyone of us girls would do. All of us girls including my stepmom were terrified. After several hours, he went to sleep it off and, reluctantly, we all slept in that bedroom we were locked in.

Well, needless to say, the next day we all left, and the summer visit was over. We were dropped off at mom's house. Dad and his new family drove back to Oklahoma.

I had heard stories about my grandfather for years, but this was the only time I witnessed anything of this nature from him. It was very terrifying.

Chapter 3

A Small Town

A Small Town

At age 15 Cindy got her driver's license. Now she could drive around, and I always had to go too. I guess Mom wanted to make sure to keep her on the straight and narrow.

Then one day, at age 13, I was riding in the back seat of my sister's car with her and her friend Elaine. We pulled up to the baseball fields to talk to two guys they knew.

Thomas and Alex came over to the car to talk to Cindy and Elaine. Both guys were good looking and much older. Thomas was very charismatic and delightful. He looked in the back seat at me and said "Well, Hello Sweetheart, you sure are a pretty little thing".

My heart just melted right then and there!! Someone had actually noticed me, and he called me "pretty"!!! From that moment on I had a super huge crush on Thomas. Every time I saw him (which was quite often in this small town) he always called my his Sweetheart or Darling. I can still hear the sound of his voice and the smell of his cologne. He also, had an infectious laugh that echoes in my head.

(More about Thomas later.)

There was also, Gary, a boy down the street from our house who would come jump on our trampoline to visit with Cindy and Elaine. He was so cute, but he never noticed me.

Sometimes we all went to the skating rink, but I would get in trouble with my sister if I would hang too close to her and her friends. Or tell on her for kissing boys.

I would go to school, come home, clean, read books and tag along with my sister, sometimes. That was my social life.

Then I made a friend named Destiny. She was pretty and funny and skinny. I would go spend the night with her sometimes and we would babysit her niece or nephew while her Mom and sister went out or worked or something. Destiny slept extremely hard and so she was not particularly good at waking up when the baby cried. Destiny was such a joy to be around. Then Destiny mentioned to me that she was in dance classes, so I told my mom I wanted to take dance classes too. I was chubby and not ballerina material, so I took tap and jazz class. Cindy and Elaine decided that they wanted to take dance class too. So, we all signed up and danced. I finally had a social life to speak of! I had an outlet, other than food, for myself.

Chapter 4

Ugly Duckling to Awkward Human

Ugly Duckling to Awkward Human

The summer before high school, I was allowed to get contacts and ditch the glasses. My hormones were changing, and my weight began to disappear. By the time school started my freshman year I was noticeably thinner and had no glasses.

I was 5 foot 8 inches tall, long blonde hair, thin and beautiful!!

The ugly duckling had been transformed into an awkward human who had no idea how to handle all the attention she was getting.

I was a new person, and everyone was shocked to see just how different I looked, but I still had no self-esteem.

All the boys began to notice me. I was not sure if it was my looks or that I was still a virgin when no one else was. I was Catholic and so I planned to stay that way. I was also still so shy for the most part and had not matured into my new -found appearance.

We still saw Thomas around town and he still called me his Sweetheart and would even give me a kiss when I saw him

About mid-way into my freshman year, Evan asked me out. (the guy who touched my hand by accident in the hallway in 7th grade)

He was tall, funny, sweet, and handsome. He had big brown eyes and brown hair. He made straight A's in school. He was so good for me. He was my rock when all the turmoil was happening at home.

My mom and Stepdad barely fought anymore, but my angry teenage sister was still rebelling about how terrible her life was.

It was a constant shouting match at our house! Cindy was sneaking out of the house or going spend the night with friends and sneaking out of their houses and doing all the things teenage girls are not supposed to do. She was also still bossing me around and taking her anger out on me with her fists and pulling my hair.

Now that my social life was a little better, I was not home much.

I spent lots of time with Evan. I still had dance lessons. I was on the drill team at school and we practiced after school and then I would go to work at the church.

On the weekends I had Friday night football games. On Saturdays I spent the night with friends and on Sunday was church. Life was better for a change.

For two years Evan and I grew remarkably close and did lots together when we had time. He was my rock amid my stormy home life.

Summers were the best because we had more time together. We would go to Evan's sister and brother in laws house. We rode horses and went shrimping and went to all kinds of festivals. (In Louisiana there is always a festival) It was awesome.

Then on New Year's Eve my cousin got married and for the rehearsal supper I had to drive her, drunk, soon to be brother in law home. When I dropped him off, he kissed me.

Needless to say, Evan found out about the kiss and after 2 years we were done. As you can imagine, I was crushed. Evan was my whole world.

To make matters worse, Evan started dating the girl who I thought was my best friend. She was the one who had told him about the kiss.

Do not get me wrong, I was not completely innocent. I did drive a drunk guy home and let him kiss me.

My world crumbled, my heart and soul were crushed. I lost my boyfriend and my friend all at the same time.

Now, all I had was more time at my toxic home. Where a person could not even think with all the arguing and fighting. My sister was constantly being punished for doing all the wrong things.

I still hung out with a few friends, but my world was never the same and I was never the same either.

That is when I started drinking, a lot. In fact, I was rather good at it. I had a high tolerance for alcohol, and I did not care.

I could out drink most of the guys. My forgotten food addiction now turned into an alcohol addiction.

I went on a few dates and had guys interested in me, but my heart was never healed from the loss of Evan.

I went to all the dances but never really dated.

I still saw Thomas around town. We would talk, hold hands, and even kiss every now and then. We even went on several dates. He was a party boy and I was a party girl, so we did fine together.

One night we even danced in the rain at a Dairy Queen, after a date. Our friends that were there even joined us after a while. It was so much fun!!

I used my neighbor's ID and, at age 17, I would sneak into the clubs to go dancing. I loved dancing and, of course, drinking.

I barely graduated school because I was just worried about partying and having fun.

At age 18 still heartbroken and lost, I lost my virginity to someone that I had known for quite a while. No one special, just someone I knew. Truth be told, he probably did not even know it was my first time.

After that, it was a spiral straight downhill. I did not care about me. I drank A LOT and partied all the time. My sister had gotten pregnant after she graduated high school and moved into the trailer park a few blocks from our house with her new baby boy. She still came over and still bossed me around when she could.

One day Cindy came over to our house and started bossing me and I would not listen to her. She started hitting me as usual when she did not get her way. Well, I really did not care and so I snapped. I grabbed her by the throat and pushed her up against the wall and told her if she ever touched me again, I would kill her. She has never touched me since that day.

Chapter 5

The Unexpected

The Unexpected

At some point after graduation our family went on vacation to my stepbrother's house in Buras, Louisiana, just south of New Orleans. While on vacation they offered for me to come stay with them after graduation, so I did.

I stayed with my stepbrother and his wife and their baby girl. I got a job at an auto parts store and began mail-in classes to become a cruise director.

I made new friends rather quickly and we partied like rock stars there too. Every weekend we went down to the liquor store bought some booze and then headed to the dam. It was an old drive in theater where all the young adults hung out because it was a small town and there was nothing else to do. We just mainly sat on the back of pickup trucks listened to music, drank, and talked.

As summer came to an end, all the friends that I had made there were making their preparations to attend college in the fall. We were checking out the colleges on weekends and the dorm rooms. We went to a couple of orientation meet and greets too. The girls that I hung out with came from money and were going to school to become Orthodontists and Lawyers. I had absolutely no direction at all. I was just living day to day, just trying to survive.

One weekend 3 of us girls decided we would go to New Orleans and see what the night life was all about near the University. We would stay at one of the girl's boyfriend's apartment. The boyfriend was a football player for Tulane University.

We all loaded our luggage in the Porsche' and headed to New Orleans. We were all dressed before we left home and went to the apartment to drop off our luggage. The first stop was the Daiquiri Hut. It was still daylight when we started our venture.

We ordered Large Octane 190s. which was 190 proof alcohol. I was used to drinking but nothing to this level. After the Daiquiri Hut we went to several clubs around town and were having a great time. At about 10:30 my 190 Octane hit me. I was drunk and needed to go lay down. The girls brought me back to the apartment, walked me up the stairs and put me to bed. They then returned to their partying.

I slept all night. At 7am I woke up to someone's hand over my mouth. He was on top of me and inside of me.

I had never seen him before and did not even know his name.

Everyone in the apartment was still asleep. There were people sleeping all over the apartment, on the floors, on the couches, in the recliners and all the beds.

I was petrified, I could not even scream! When he was done, I got up and went to the bathroom, where I took a long hot shower and cried the entire time. I got dressed and went and sat in a chair in the living room until everyone woke up. I never saw that awful boy again. Nor did I ever tell anyone. I was devastated and embarrassed.

A few weeks later I heard from a friend that he was bragging to people that he had sex with me.

I denied it and told everyone that he was a liar and that I would never have sex with him.

I did not want my new friends to know that he had raped me.

After this I stopped caring about life, even more. I started drinking even more and started my old habit of comfort eating too.

It was around this time that my Dad was going through a divorce from his second wife, who was leaving him for his best friend. (Boy could I relate to that) He needed me for moral support. Dad moved to Westlake into an apartment in town. So, I moved back in with Mom in Westlake so that I would be closer to him.

I continued to drink and eat like there was no tomorrow. I would even go have a drink of scotch or bourbon with my Dad every day.

Then Dad found a new girlfriend and got back on his way.

After a while, a girl I knew from high school and I moved to Austin, Texas. We shared an apartment for a few months then I got a job and rented my own apartment. I lived there for a little over a year. I was not old enough to go out but the women I made friends within my apartment complex was 30 years old and knew all the right people to get me in. I continued to party like crazy.

The company I worked for shut down and then my car broke down and so, I was done in Austin. I sold my car to a junk yard. My cousin, and his friend, drove to with a trailer to load all my furniture up and bring me back to Louisiana.

I moved back into Mom's house with the baby sister and stepdad. I would hang out with friends on the weekends, still drinking and eating.

I got a job at a convenience store on the corner by our house.

One weekend, around Christmas time, I went to the club to dance and who did I see, it was Thomas. Thomas had gone to South Carolina for a job and was in town for the weekend. He had kept his home here for the time being.

As always, when I saw Thomas, he greeted me with his sexy little "Hello Sweetheart" and a kiss. He grabbed me and said, "Let's go dance". We danced all night long, until the club shut down which was at 2am. We had the best time ever! He offered breakfast, so we went to a little diner and had breakfast and then he offered me to come back to his place. So, I did.

When we got to Thomas's house his brother, Jerry was there watching tv. We talked with him for a little while and then headed to the bedroom on the other end of the house.

We had several years of mutual attraction built up and we let it all loose. We made love all night long. Up until this point, it was the best night of my life.

The next few days were Christmas festivities. We spent all the time we could together. He even bought me a jewelry box for Christmas. Then came the time he had to go back to South Carolina. We talked for hours and he tried to talk me into moving there with him. As bad as I wanted to do that, I knew I would have a fight on my hands. My mother would never allow that to happen.

With much sorrow in my heart, I said no. This would turn out to be one of the biggest regrets ever in my life.

I was devastated and this put me even more in a depression, not caring about what happened to me. I continued to work and hang out with my friends.

Three months later I found out that Thomas had gotten back together with the girl he broke up with before he came home for Christmas and that they were engaged. Apparently, she claimed that she was pregnant.

About a couple weeks after finding this out, I found out that I was pregnant. I did not tell anyone who the baby was for. I once again was crushed, hurt and all alone. Added bonus, I now had a baby on the way to consider.

I was about 6 months pregnant when a mutual friend of Thomas and I figured out who the baby was for and told me I needed to tell him. He was now planning a wedding and the girl he was marrying had "lost" the baby.

So, I made a phone call to Thomas to tell him that I was pregnant. He was incredibly quiet on the phone and then asked if I was sure it belonged to him. I said yes, absolutely. That is when he broke down and cried. He was in between a rock and a hard place. He was getting married and it was too late. He asked me what I wanted, and I told him just to provide the baby with health insurance and that I did not want anything else from him.

So, here I was. My Mom was furious with me. I was still not giving anyone the name of the father. There were only a couple of people that knew. Lots of friends and family tried talking to me about adoption and abortion. I just could not even think about it. First of all, I would never be able to kill the child. Secondly, no one could love this baby the way I could.

So, on September 8th, 1986, Savannah entered this world as a premature 4-pound baby girl. Savannah got her name from a show I watched, while I was pregnant. It was called Savannah Smiles. I had no idea at the time that Thomas worked at the Savannah River Power Plant. I learned that later.

Due to complications, Savannah was born 20 days early. She was so tiny it was scary, and she had every pediatric specialist in the area checking on her. They started asking questions on her family history, while I knew my side, I did not know anything about the family history on Thomas's side. It was then that the family friend who knew who the father was called his Mom and told her we needed information for the doctors. Thomas's mom, Mrs. Betty, and Thomas's brother Jerry came to visit at the hospital and gave the doctors all the information needed. Jerry was there the night me and Thomas got together so I am sure he told his mom. When Mrs. Betty left, she called Thomas and told him to call me at the hospital. The following afternoon Thomas did call, and we talked for an exceedingly long time. We laughed and joked and talked all about Savannah. He even told me a story that he and his wife were watching a movie the night before and it was about a guy having a baby with a surrogate mother and his wife on the same day. Thomas's wife, looked at him, she was now 6 months pregnant, and said, "if you ever do that, I will kill you." Thomas said all he could think about was me at the hospital having Savannah. He said he just wanted to climb behind the couch and disappear but just played it off. Thomas's wife still did not know anything about me or Savannah.

Because of being so small she had to gain weight before leaving the hospital, Savannah was in the hospital for 9 days. I was a nervous wreck. Some of the specialists did not speak English very well and I could not understand what they were telling me. My fever and blood pressure kept going up and down, so I had to stay in the hospital with her. That was probably best.

When I took Savannah home, she would stay up around the clock, except for little cat naps. It appeared that the nurses on the day and night shift, loved on her around the clock and so she did not know morning from night. Mom and I would take turns with her so that we could both get some sleep. Savannah was spoiled very quickly because she was so tiny and cute.

Four weeks after giving birth, I went to work on a turnaround out at the refinery. I had to take the job because I had no other options. My hours were 4:30am to 6pm. I needed money for diapers and formula. Savannah was too tiny to breastfeed, and formula was expensive.

At first Savannah would stay with Mom while I worked. Mom had Savannah all the time because I had started going out again. It grew to be much more than mom wanted to handle. So, after a while, I hired a sitter for when I was at work.

Chapter 6

Life Changes

Life Changes

Then I met Shonda!

Shonda was a newly divorced single mom who lived in Sulphur. She was quiet and did not like being alone. Shonda and I started hanging out and doing things together. Her sister-in-law was in high school and she would babysit for us. When Shonda and I would hang out we would always have a great time together.

After a while, Shonda offered for me and Savannah to move in with her and her young daughter, Faith. Savannah and I could have Faith's room and Shonda would let Faith sleep with her.

It was perfect. Savannah and Faith would play together and me and Shonda would hang out.

My job on the turnaround ended and I got a regular 8am to 5pm job. Savannah continued to go to the sitter while I worked and every now and then mom would take Savannah for a night or two. On the weekends Shonda and I would clean house and then go have fun and her sister-in-law would babysit for us. We always got into a lot of shenanigans and would always laugh and enjoy our life.

We had a great thing going. We had friends that would come over and grill for us. We had people inviting us to events. We knew lots of people and were having the time of our lives.

One night a friend of Shonda's, Kerry, introduced me to a tall and handsome guy. I talked with him a little that night while we were out. I told Shonda I was not sure he was for me. He seemed a little arrogant. Kerry told Shonda that the guy, Stewart, was extremely interested in me and I should give him another chance. After a little persuasion from Shonda and Kerry, I gave Stewart another shot and went on a date with him. This time he seemed more caring and not so self-centered. We actually had real conversations and hit it off. He was much sweeter with the one on one date, than he had been in the group of friends.

We started dating on a regular basis. We went to Houston and spent the weekend with his mom. We dined at the restaurant where his mom worked, and all seemed good. After months of dating, Stewart ask me to move in with him. Shonda tried to talk me out of it. She saw something about him that she did not like, and she could not explain it, but she knew.

Of course, I did not listen, and Stewart and I moved in together with Savannah. We rented a small house in Westlake to start out.

After several months' things began to change a bit. He was very jealous and had a slight temper sometimes. He would also make small remarks to make me doubt myself that were just not quite right. He asked me to marry him one night at dinner and I said no that I was not feeling it.

I told him that his temper made me uncomfortable. We continued to live together, and he was on good behavior because he still wanted me to marry him.

A few months later, I found out that I was pregnant. Of course, he was excited and wanted to marry me right away. I gave in and married him. We took off work early one day and went down to the courthouse and now my wagon was hitched to his.

Shortly into the marriage, the verbal abuse began. He began saying I was fat, (which I assure you I was not, my tummy was flat even up to 6 months of pregnancy) I wasn't allowed to talk to anyone, even family members, without him around. He was an EXTREMLY jealous person. It became worse and worse as time progressed, but this is what I had seen growing up arguing and fighting were almost normal. At night he would get dressed and go to the bar, leaving me at home with no vehicle. When it got closer to time for the baby to be born, we moved to an apartment in Sulphur behind the post office.

I had gotten a job at a Case equipment dealership and he worked construction. He mostly just worked 6 months out of the year, and I worked to keep us afloat. On June 5th, 1989 Martin was born.

We were the happy little family (to the outside world). I was still getting verbally abused at home and he was still leaving me home with the kids while he went out to drink beer at the bar.

I eventually borrowed some money from my Grandparents, and we bought an old trailer and a 5-acre piece of land in the country.

When we moved to the country, I thought things would tone down, but they actually got worse. That is when he began to physically abuse me. He would also pawn things when he was not working and wanted money. He pawned all my rings one day while I was at work. Then he never went to get them out. One was a pearl ring that my grandfather had given to my mother, one was my class ring, and then there was a sapphire ring a friend had given me in high school. It was always turmoil, and there was never any peace.

After 3 years, I had had enough and was determined that I was going to leave him. Then, as luck would have it …. I discovered I was pregnant again. I cursed him for weeks. He would call me on the phone, and I would curse him. He would walk in the door at home and I would curse him. Finally, we had a conversation and he promised that he would be a better person to me. He talked me into staying with him saying that he would change, which he did for a while.

When I was about 7 ½ months pregnant we were having an argument and he pushed me so hard into the dresser that I ended up with a bruise the size of a basketball on my pregnant belly. I cried often until I gave birth, just hoping that it had not hurt my poor innocent baby.

One night he got mad at me, put me in my bedroom, and shut the door. A few minutes later he came and threw the garbage from the kitchen on top of me and I was covered in garbage and he would not let me out. Hours later I was allowed to go clean myself up in the bathroom. Then I still had to wash my sheets and mop my room. He told me he just wanted me to feel like trash.

On December 1st, 1990 I gave birth to a beautiful baby boy, Michael, and he was perfect!! Ten fingers and ten toes. He had a great disposition. With all the stress and with all the abuse I was very thin, especially for having had 3 children I was always a nervous wreck and began to worry about my health.

Stewart. would rarely give me money for bills. Every now and then he would give me money for groceries. If I needed milk for my babies, I would have to sneak money out of his truck, while he was passed out. I would never take more than 5 dollars (just enough for milk). I did get caught a couple of times and he would beat me and call me names.

When Michael was about 8 months old, I had had enough. I hated the sight of the man that had abused me for so long. My decision was made.

One afternoon as the children played in their room, I told my husband that it was over, and I wanted a divorce. He picked me up and threw me on the couch. My head hit the cushioned arm of the couch, hard. It hurt so bad. I placed my hand on the back of my head and when I pulled it away and we saw blood, he immediately began to apologize. He swore that it would never happen again and told me how much he "loved" me.

I waited about a week and I went home early from work, packed some clothes for me and my children. The kids and I moved into my old bedroom at Mom's house. I used the twin bed in the room, and I made a pallet on the floor for my young children. We ended up staying there for several months because my husband refused to leave my house. He had no credit and basically never wanted to contribute any money so everything was in my name. I was paying all the bills. I filed for divorce and I had to wait for the officials to evict him. The day before he was evicted, he called me at mom's and said he had turned the gas on and was going to kill himself and burn down the house in the process. I knew he loved himself more than anything so he could never go through with it. I was terribly upset with the whole divorce and this did not help matters at all, but I stood my ground. I told him "Good luck with that." and hung up the phone.

On November 1st Me and my children moved back into our house. I must have cleaned for an entire week straight. It smelt like gas from the stove, which is what he used to try to "burn the house down" and it smelled like him, too. I wiped down walls, mopped the floors, and cleaned everything in that house. It took me a whole week, cleaning every day, to get it to smell nice.

It was peaceful and tranquil for the first time ever.

Chapter 7

It Is not Over Yet

It Is not Over

One day in late January my almost ex-husband showed up at my house and refused to leave. He was trying to convince me that in the divorce we should each get custody of one of our boys. He told me that if we each took a child then no one would owe the other child support. I was not having it, but I said, "Well which son would you take?" He said, "It doesn't matter, just pick one." I was so angered that he would even ask me to part with any of my children, much less to "just pick one". I told him it was not happening and that he needed to leave, but he refused. I had to eventually call the police and get them to make him leave. One of the officers told Stewart. that he never wanted him to come back to my house again. It was at that time that the police officer told me that it would be best to include a restraining order in with my divorce paperwork. So, I had my lawyer draw up the paperwork and did just that.

A couple weeks later, in early February, I was home alone with my children. My children were asleep. I was watching the playback footage of the Mardi Gras parade that had taken place earlier that evening. I got a phone call from a guy I had been introduced to by a mutual friend. He asked if he could come watch the parade with me. I told him that was fine.

The guy, I do not even remember his name anymore, was there for about 15 minutes when I saw headlights in my driveway. I looked out of the front window and saw my soon to be ex-husband. I immediately picked up the phone to dial 911 but Stewart had already broken into the locked front door and jerked the phone out of the wall.

Stewart then proceeded to attack the guy. Somehow, the guy finally got away, ran out the back door and left. Stewart's fury then with nowhere left to turn, turned towards me. I was punched everywhere imaginable, pulled down the long hallway by my hair, thrown against walls, kicked in the face with his cowboy boots, pulled back down the hallway by my hair, and thrown to the living room floor. He then proceeded to sit on top of me trying to choke the life out of me. I knew right then and there that I was about to die. By this time, my young children had woken up and were in the hallway crying and screaming. I was determined that I could not let my kids see me die this way, all the while, praying for God's help.

I do not know where else the answer came from, if not from God. I looked at the man that was trying to kill me and said, "I didn't know you loved me this much" He immediately stopped what he was doing and said "What?" I repeated my statement and he said "Yes, now you get it". I told him "Let me go put the kids back to bed and calm them down and we will talk about it." He said "No, I'll put them back to bed". So, I let him.

As soon as he got down the long hallway, I looked out the front door and the police were driving by my house. I ran, as fast as I could, across my yard. I jumped the ditch and flagged them down from the road.

The police officers came back, and I told them what happened. Of course, they could see the bruises on my face, body, and neck, so it was obvious I was telling the truth.

As luck would have it, the officer that had told Stewart. to never come back to my house and told me to file the restraining order, was one of the officers on duty that night. He was so mad but showed remarkable restraint. You could tell he wanted to beat the life out of Stewart. As Stewart was crying and begging me not to press charges the police officer kept telling him "shut up and look at what you have done to her face." I am sure if it would have been different circumstances the officer would have beat Stewart senseless, but the officer was very professional.

Stewart was arrested and put in the back of the patrol car.

The next day I had to go to the Sheriff's office so that photos could be taken of all my bruises all over my body and face. Eventually Stewart went to court, paid some court fines and fees, and he was done. It was probably 6 months later when Stewart showed up at a designated mutual meeting place to pick up the boys for his weekend visit. He gave me a 22-shot gun and said that he wanted me to have it because he knew I would use it. He told me that he never wanted to do that to me again.

It was shortly after this that I was out with a girl that I worked with and her husband. I was introduced to Casey, a guy they knew. Casey was overly sweet, handsome and could not take his eyes off me as we all had a conversation. He asked me to dance and we talked all night and just hung out with our friends. Casey asked me if I would go out on a date with him. He was separated from his wife at the time and filing for divorce. I agreed to go out with him the following week. Monday morning when I showed up for work, I had a dozen long stem roses delivered to me. Just because I said yes to go out with him! I was not used to such grand gestures and thought I was in heaven. We had several dates and hung out a lot. One night we were at Mom's house watching tv with my little sister when a car drove up in the driveway. We looked out the window and saw Stewart putting a rose on my windshield. He had been out and bought a rose for me at the bar. We all went outside, and Casey met him at his truck. Stewart was going to get out of his truck when Casey pushed him back in using the door of the truck. He told Stewart that if he stepped out of the truck, he would get an ass whooping. Stewart stayed in the truck and drove off.

Casey and I dated for a few months until one day, he told me that his soon to be ex-wife wanted to try and make their marriage work. So, Casey went back to her and tried to make it work for his son. I could not be upset with him for trying to keep his family together. Although, I was alone and crushed again.

We did keep in touch and even met up every now and then. His marriage did not work out, but our timing never matched up again. Either I was dating when he was single or vice versa. We are still friends to this day. After this, I had a date occasionally, but nothing serious. I was scared of men and I was in man hater-mode. Stewart's abuse had left me very hurt, afraid, and untrusting toward.

One Friday afternoon I was dropping my boys off with their dad for the weekend. As I was leaving with my window down, telling my boys I loved them and I would see them on Sunday, I heard Stewart say "You probably going to the bar, you Bitch" He only said this because the two guys that had dropped him off from work were still in the driveway. I was so fuming mad. Here was the man that went to the bar almost every night the whole time we were married, and HE was belittling ME!! Well, I put my car in drive and parked it right back in his driveway. I got out of my car and walked straight back onto the front porch and I said, "What did you call me?" He said, "You heard me, Bitch" I said, "You need to apologize." He told me there was no way he was going to apologize to me. That is when I reached down and grabbed him between his legs. His eyes got a little large and he said, "What are you doing?" I said, "You are going to apologize to me." We went back and forth with this argument several times and each time he refused I squeezed a little tighter.

Finally, when my nails were dug into my hand as tight as I could squeeze, and he was down on his knees. In a high pitch voice, he whispered "Ok, ok I'm sorry" I said, "I can't hear you." So then, he yelled "OK I'M SORRY!!" I released my grip and said "Thank you and have a great weekend" I got back in my car and left.

A few months later. I went to listen to a band with my next-door neighbors, Marie, and her husband Karl. I left the table to go to the restroom. As I was exiting the restroom a gentleman said, "Excuse me, Is your name Donna?" I said "Yes, but. I'm sorry, I don't know you" and I kept walking. He stopped me again and said "I know you don't know me, but I was at Stewart's house the day you put him on his knees on the front porch. I turned ten shades of red and was so embarrassed. I covered my face with my hands, and I said "Oh my, I'm so sorry. I normally do not do things like that, but he just got on my last nerve after all he has done to me" The guy said "Oh do not worry about it. That has got to be the funniest thing I have ever seen." The gentleman proceeded to tell me that they make fun of Stewart every day at work about it. This guy introduced himself as Steve and asked me to dance. We danced several times that night. After that night, if I saw Steve anywhere, he would come get me to dance. I continue to hang out with my friends and go dancing.

My neighbors, Marie, and Karl were a God sent piece of heaven. Our children hung out together. My daughter fell right in between their daughters in age and their son fell right in between my sons in age.

The kids played together, and we would barbeque and have bonfires all the time. We had lots of people that would come over on the weekends with their kids. We had volleyball nets set up and we even had tournaments. Our houses always had shenanigans going on. We did Christmas caroling with all our neighbors. I would make big pots of gumbo and lots of hot chocolate. The neighbor across the pasture would pile hay on a trailer and we all loaded up and went all around in the country singing to the neighbors.

When we did not have company, I would go over to have coffee or margaritas with Marie. It was a great peaceful time in our lives.

We had neighbors that had a rodeo arena in their back yard, so we also attended the rodeos with our kiddos. We all have lots of special memories from those days. I did go out with a young guy. He was cute and sweet, but he claimed I had too many kids. Then, I started seeing a police officer, Phil, who would have been the perfect catch, had I not still been in man hater mode. I was not mentally ready to trust another man or get too serious. I called him "Phil me" as a joke. His buddies thought it was funny and so did my friends. Phil was a wonderful guy with a great disposition. We had lots of fun together. We are still friends.

Chapter 8

Let's Try again

Let's Try again

After 4 years of being single and hating men, I began to think I did not want to spend the rest of my life alone. I was fixed up on a blind date by my little sisters' new husband. It was a guy that he knew and went fishing with all the time. The first night we all met at a restaurant and then went out dancing. We had fun but I really did not think he was my type. I actually thought he was too "preppy" for me. I was persuaded by my sister and brother in law to "give him a chance." So, I did. His name was Marshall and he was a very cute, nice, and funny guy. After I got to know him, Marshall was not preppy at all. He began coming over every day. On the weekends, when he was off work, Marshall would take me and all the kids fishing, swimming or whatever we wanted to do. It was all about me and my children. He helped me around the house with dishes and cooking. This was a great thing and it was working out. We were always doing things with the kids and with other couples. We were enjoying life. After 4 months he proposed. What was not to love? I was finally making a family for my children. Several months after taking marriage classes and all the things that come with it, we were married. Since I had eloped for my first marriage, I had the big church wedding. The night of our wedding Marshall even carried me over the threshold.

Later that year, on November 10th, 1995 I had another baby boy, Joseph. He was a little stinker and he was spoiled. We spoiled him and even my other children spoiled him.

Marshall seemed very kind and loving. We never fought or argued. He worked three jobs but always made time for me and the kids. We did everything as a family. Several months into our marriage he told me he was going fishing, several times in a row, with some friends. I asked him, after a while, when he was going to spend time with the family. His response was "You my ole lady now. I don't have to spend time with you." Well, we had a "come to Jesus" about that little comment. First of all, I am NOT anyone's "ole lady" and secondly now is when you should be spending time with the family.

So, that never happened again. After some time, his 3 jobs slowly turned into no jobs. He was unemployed and not even searching for work. He just wanted to fish or hunt every day. I finally sat him down and told him that he needed to get a job. His response to me was "Well you did it all before I came along, so what's the difference now?" That is when I told him that the difference now was that I was not his mother and he needed to contribute to our household if he wanted to be in this family. He then decided to get a job as a hunting and fishing guide. That only lasted until hunting season was over. Then he was back to no job at all.

We remained friends but after 4 ½ years we separated. We would still do things together. We went canoeing and fishing with friends. I was thinking that this was temporary until he got the whole "job" thing straightened out and pulled himself together.

Then came the awful day that I learned he had molested one of my boys. I would have never, ever, ever thought this about him. He was a big flirt and I would have thought he would have cheated on me before I would have thought this. Anyone that knew him also found it hard to believe.

The day I found out Marshall had Joseph with him at a hunting lease for the weekend, I called him on the phone. It was Saturday. I said, "bring my baby home now." Marshall asked me what was wrong and all I could say was "bring my baby home now."

I called my Mom and told her what I had found out and that I was going to kill him. She told me I could not. I told her "if I can shoot a deer at 150 yards, and kill it, then I could sure kill him." She told me that she knew I was capable but that I should not. As much as my mother disliked him, she talked me out of killing him. She told me to let the justice system do their job. I know mom had an ulterior motive. She knew if I went to jail, she would end up with my kids. So, I did not kill him. I was very protective over my kids. I would not even let them watch regular TV most of the time, because there was too much trash on television. We had lots of Disney movies and we watched them often.

Marshall brought my baby home and I met them on the front porch. I told Joseph to kiss his dad goodbye and go in the house. That is when I told Marshall to sit down and I told him what I had learned. He tried to talk loud and bold and intimidate me into not believing what I had heard. I told Marshall to get in his car and to leave or I would kill him with my bare hands. To tell you the truth I probably could have, I was so mad, hurt, and disgusted. He hung his head and got in his car and left. When he did, I called the Sheriff's department and turned him in.

Marshall was arrested, booked, and let out on bail. He failed his lie detector test. His excuse was that he was nervous and on Xanax.

My children all had to go in for evaluation and counseling to see who knew what. They also had to go in front of the Grand Jury. The whole ordeal was a long drawn out process.

Marshall started dating while we were going through the whole process and leading up to the trial. By the time he went to trial and was convicted, his girlfriend was 7 months pregnant. He was sentenced to prison for 15 years. He had a stack of letters from people he knew, on his outstanding reputation. He even asked me to write a letter in his defense. What nerve!! It ended up that with good behavior and reduced sentence he only had to serve 5 years.

Chapter 9

And Again

And Again

As this long drawn out court and sentencing ordeal was going on, a family friend, David (most people called him Dave) would come to court with me. I did not want to be alone with that monster that had violated my children and I's whole life. David had worked with Pop. I had known him for years. We started hanging out even when I did not have court to go to. He would go to the grocery store and buy a ton of groceries and show up to my house to drop them off. David was 18 years older than I was. I had worked with him when I was about 19 years old and had never had any issues with him. I thought he was very mature and had himself together. David always treated me sweet and kind. We started dating after my ex-husband was sentenced to prison. We mostly went to one of his son's houses for barbeques. We hung out at home a lot and cooked. He also liked to cook so, that was our thing. Every now and then he had a little attitude, but after all I had been through so far, a little attitude was nothing. I worked for his son and I loved my job. I did break up with him once because he was very rude to me. After a while, he worked his way back and we had no problems. After us dating for a while, he got an opportunity to work in the U.S. Virgin Islands as a consultant. He told me he wanted me to go with him and he wanted to marry me. I agreed to marry him but with us leaving town all the time, I could not do the job I was doing. So, I had to give my notice at work.

We put the plan into motion. We planned a nice western wedding with all our friends and family in attendance. The wedding was fabulous, and everyone had a great time. That night, at midnight, we headed to the airport and flew to St. Croix for our honeymoon. David had rented a condo there for work and that is where we stayed. He went to work while I was there, and we would do things in the evening when he would get off. I stayed a week and got to know a lot of the other wives.

The plan was for me and the children to move to the island during summer and we were to all live as a family. However, when we all went for the summer, we began to learn it was not that easy.

The public schools in St. Croix, which is a U.S. Virgin island, are not accredited in the States. All my children would have to attend a private school which cost $1500.00 per student each year. I had 4 children and that would have been too much. It also would be my daughter's senior year at high school. So, after much discussion and planning, it was decided. David would stay on the island and my children and I would go back home after the summer. The kids would go to school back in Sulphur. I still had my home in the country so that is what we did. My children were happy to return home.

With school activities, my boys played every kind of ball there was football, baseball, basketball, and soccer, we stayed busy all the time. After a while, David began to get jealous. Although, my friends on the island said he was always at the casino or out with friends. David wanted to know where I was and what I was doing all the time. I did not have a problem with that, and I would tell him.

One night I was at dinner with 3 friends, all girls. We went to a Mexican restaurant and were ordering food when David called. I answered the phone and he started yelling at me. "What are you doing at the bar?" I said, "I am at Peppers Mexican restaurant" He again accused me of being at a bar because the music was so loud. I told him that I was not even sitting in the bar area. I was in the main dining area. He did not believe me and was mad.

After this episode, and a few more like it, my "give a damn" was slowly but surely getting busted. Especially, when he would yell at me. I had sat him down several times and told him that if he did not stop yelling at me, I would eventually end our marriage because my heart would be broken.

At that time, I was also having some female issues. I had already had a tubal surgery a year earlier. Now, I was suffering with excruciating pain and lots of bleeding. What is worse is, I never knew when I would bleed. There was no time frame for this. Sometimes I would have to catch myself because the stabbing pain in my legs would make me almost fall. I planned a trip to visit my husband and thought maybe this would ease his mind. It just so happened that, on the plane ride there, it hit me. My pain was intense, and the bleeding started too. It takes a whole day with switching planes in Florida and Porta Rico, to get to St. Croix. I was exhausted and in pain when I arrived. He was so very mad at me when I would not have sex with him that night, that we had a huge fight. He pitched a fit like a two-year-old child.

We ended the trip on a better note, and all was good again, for a while.

I eventually had to have surgery for my issues. I had a total hysterectomy and they even removed some adhesions. My husband opted not to come home and be with me during the surgery. He told me he would come home in a few months when I was feeling better so we could spend some time together.

I went in for surgery and, as always, my family members took care of my children. I actually stayed in the hospital for days. The doctors could not get me to stop running fever and throwing up. After several days it was under control and they sent me home. When I got discharged from the hospital, Mom dropped me off at home. Two hours later I began to throw up again. There was so much, I did not think I had that much fluid in my body. I had to call my mom to come bring me back to the hospital. After another day they inserted a tube down into my stomach to keep me from throwing up.

One of the wives, whose husband was working in St. Croix, came by the hospital to check on me. She could not believe her eyes. When she left the hospital, she called her husband, JC. She told JC to tell David to get on the next plane and come check on his wife. She told him that I was very pale and looked like I was about to die. That is exactly how I felt too. That next day David was at the hospital and stayed by my side. After 9 days total of being in the hospital I was discharged and feeling much better. David decided that since I was out of the hospital and doing better that he would go to West Texas for 3 days and go deer hunting with some friends. So, he did. When he returned from Texas, for the next few days, at least, we went riding around shopping for land to buy in the country. He wanted 10 to 20 acres and I only had 5 acres on my property.

Then after only a week and a half he flew back to St. Croix and went back to work. My job while he was gone, was to continue to shop for more property. We were back to getting along (for the most part). He could be an ass occasionally, but I could tolerate his little attitude.

I eventually found some property in Singer, La. David and I arranged a deal that he would save the Per diem he was paid to pay the note on the land that was due every six months. I was in charge of his paycheck and I was paying off all his bills from before we were married. He also had to pay child support for his daughter, as well as for all other extracurricular activities. He was also paying on his ex-wife's car. On one of the trip's David made to come home, we sold his truck (which I had finally managed to pay off) and traded my car in on a Ford F250 King Ranch edition. He really wanted that truck, so we got it. This truck cost more than I had paid for my house and my land combined. It was nice and had all the bells and whistles.

It was also on this trip that he asked me where I was spending the money, after he spent all day at the local casino. I had a notebook, with all the bills and payments, that I showed to him and he said ok and that he was just checking.

After he returned to the island for work, we would call each other several times a day to catch up on what was going on. One day as I was talking to David on the phone, I mentioned to him that the land note would be due in about a month. It was then that he told me he had not saved his money and he did not have the money to pay the note. He told me I should pay it with the money from his check. I explained to him we did not have the money because we had just paid off his truck and spent $3,000 on a deer lease membership he wanted, not to make mention all the credit cards I was paying off.

It was at that time that he started cursing me. After several minutes, I hung up the phone. David called back a few moments later and asked, "Did you hang up on me?". I said "Yes, I did, and I will again if you start cursing at me". He said, "I wasn't cursing at you". I said, "You were talking to me and cursing and that is why I hung up." He told me "I wasn't cursing AT you; I was just cursing. You just happened to be on the phone".

Regardless if he was cursing to me or at me, he was slowly busting my "give a damn" a little more. At this point I was trying to figure out how I was going to afford to be single again. I did not have a job, and the $200 car note I had, was now $1900. for this fancy truck that David just had to have.

I had a friend that owned a carpet store and had been asking me to help her out. I decided that a part time job would allow me to have some money of my own and to open my own savings account. So, I started selling carpet and I had a lot of fun working with my friend.

Now I was working during the day and in the evenings, I was cooking, cleaning, and bringing my kids to whatever activities they happened to be involved in.

My daughter had a field trip for school and had to meet the bus at 5 am one morning. We woke up at 4am and I drove her to meet the bus. Then I went back home to get ready for work and get the boys off to school. After school, the boys had ball games and then I still had to cook supper. We got to bed late. Early the next morning again I had to meet the field trip bus to pick up my daughter. Then it was back home to get everyone ready for school and me ready for work. We had ball games again this night, and we were getting to bed late. The next day everyone went off to school and work. After work I came home and fed the children. Some of my friends called and wanted me to come meet them for a drink. I told them I was exhausted, but they persisted.

So, I said I would only have one drink and I had to get some sleep.

I met up with my friends, had 2 drinks and talked with a lot of other friends we saw there. At about 9:30 I headed home. Somewhere along the way I fell asleep at the wheel. My truck went into the ditch and hit a huge oak tree that was growing there. My airbag deployed and I woke up to see flames coming out from under the hood on the passenger side of the vehicle. I grabbed my purse, got out of the car, and called 911. I told the dispatch operator what happened and that I needed the police and a fire truck. The police and fire department responded. By the time they arrived my truck was engulfed in flames. I told the police officer exactly what happened, and he did not write me a ticket, just an accident report.

I had a full tank of diesel fuel and the truck burned down to the metal. The officer sent me home. I called my neighbor to come pick me up. After the fire department put the fire out, the policeman delivered the accident paperwork to me at home. The truck was a total loss.

The next morning, I called my insurance adjuster. With much sincerity he asked me if I am injured and if I am ok? Then told me not to worry and the insurance would take care of me. He said that he was glad that I was not hurt.

The next phone call I made, was to my husband. He said "What the hell? How is the truck and how much damage was done?" I told him that the truck was totaled, and he started a cursing rant. I hung up on him.

When my husband called back and asked if I hung up on him. I said "Yes!" My husband then asked me why I had hung up on him. I then explained to David that the insurance guy, whom I had only seen three times in my entire life, was more concerned about my well-being than my own husband was. At this moment he asks me "Well are you ok?" This only confirmed, in my mind, what I had been thinking for some time now. It was at that point that I was truly done with him. I wanted nothing more to do with his selfish tantrums and cursing. I told him that I wanted a divorce. This truck had become a curse to make me stay in this marriage and now it was gone. Thank you, Jesus!!!!

I called my mom to come pick me up and take me to the car lot. I needed to find a vehicle. She asked me if I wanted to wait for my husband and I said no. I used my own credit information and I registered the car in my name only.

It takes a whole day to get to Louisiana from St. Croix. David was at the house the very next morning. He knocked on the door (even though he had a key) and I let him in. We talked a while and I told him I was done with all the cursing and hollering. I told him I wanted a divorce. After only one year, it was over. He was pissed and started packing his clothes into trash bags. The more he packed the madder he got. He threw a trash bag down at one point and said, "You just pack my shit and I'll be back to get it tomorrow" Then he left.

The following morning, I was outside with my dog, Dakota, (a rottweiler David insisted we have). David drove up in a rental car. He came walking up and asked me if I had packed his shit. I said "No". His eyes lit up and I could tell he was a little happier just to hear that. He asked, "Why not?" So, I said "Well, as far as I'm concerned, you're a fucking grown ass man and you can pack it your damn self" He really got pissed then. He said, "Well then just burn the damn shit" I said "ok" and he left in a hurry.

The next morning, I was served with divorce papers. David told me to find a lawyer and that he would pay for it, to change my last name. David said I did not deserve his last name. I told him to get a lawyer and pay for it, because I did not care I was not getting married again anytime soon. He did not get the lawyer or put a specific request in the divorce papers. 15 years later I still have his last name. I am sure it still makes him mad.

Chapter 10

Happiness

Happiness

After my separation, I mostly hung out with my girlfriends as before. One Wednesday afternoon, I went to the local Mexican Restaurant to meet the girls for happy hour. I was the first to arrive so, I reserved a large table in the bar area. I was sitting at the table waiting on my friends when a guy approached the jukebox near me and said "Excuse me, can you help me play some music? My contacts are blurry, and I can't see the song names." I helped him pick out some music and told him that I was waiting for my wild and crazy girlfriends. He laughed and said that he was waiting for his wild and crazy guy friends also. He sat at the table right next to mine and we talked as we waited for our friends to arrive. As we talked, I learned that his name was Dave, this is what everyone called my ex-husband. When I told him that my name was Donna, I learned that was his ex-wife's name. How ironic is that!!

After we learned this, it was our little joke.

I thought to myself, "why can't I ever just meet a nice guy like that? He just had the "nice guy" vibe to him. When all our friends arrived, I knew a couple of his friends and we all enjoyed each other's company. After happy hour we all went to a local Pub and went dancing. We all had crazy, belly laughing, fun that night. He asked me out for coffee and breakfast. I was not going to go but our mutual friend Casey told me that he was a nice guy and it was ok, and that Dave was harmless. So, we had breakfast and he asked me for my number, which surprised me. We began hanging out all the time and eventually began to date. After a year he moved in with me. Dave played music and was a great Trumpet player. My nickname for him was "Trumpet Lips". I went to many of his gigs and met a lot of great people.

Dave was the sweetest kindest man I had been with in a long time. He treated me well and was truly kind. He even called me a Princess. He would draw my bath water at night and bring me a glass of wine in the tub. He would cook for me and the kids. If I had an overnight trip for work, he would meet me in the driveway at my truck to unload my suitcase. He would tell me that supper was cooked, and I could either eat first or take a bath because he had my tub ready for me. And he would bring me a glass of wine in the tub. Whatever I wanted was fine with him. We were fabulous together. I had a major hang up with men at this time, of course. I would not let him tell me he loved me. Words meant nothing to me. We got along perfectly, and he was so good for me.

After being together for 4 years, the unthinkable happened. We were out of town; he was playing music out in the middle of nowhere in a little restaurant/club. When we left that place and got near the interstate where we had cell service again, my phone was dinging with tons of messages and missed calls. This was strange because I normally did not get any messages or phone calls. This would become the worst night of my life.

Chapter 11

Total Devastation

Total Devastation

I finally got in touch with one of my friends, who automatically asked to talk to Dave. This was also strange because she did not know him that well. Dave had to break the news to me that my 17-year-old son, Martin had been in a car accident. My son had not survived. All the wind was sucked out of my sails and I was an empty vessel at this point. I hit rock bottom with no way up. We drove straight to the hospital, where I was informed by the police officers of what had happened and got the details on viewing the body, of my now deceased son. I also went upstairs to visit the girl that had been driving and was now in critical condition. I was then faced with planning a funeral for my son and could barely even catch my breath. It was and still is the hardest thing I have ever had to deal with.

Dave was by my side through the entire process. He was my rock in this terrible time.

I called my work to see if I had life insurance on Martin

Mandy, the Human Resource director, told me that I had filled out all the paperwork but had not signed that portion of the paperwork. She said, "I'm so sorry Donna". It was what it was, and I could not change it, now.

I made a phone call to my Best friend, Marie, who had moved and lived out of state. Marie immediately took off driving to Louisiana. I also made a phone call to my friend, Debbie, who lived in the neighboring city. She was at my house within minutes. Debbie took control she drove us to all the places I needed to be to make the necessary arrangements, the funeral home, and the graveyard. We also stopped by the site where the wreck had occurred. Debbie also suggested that I open a bank account for donations to help with burial cost. I agreed this was a good idea. So, Debbie called the bank and arranged for the account to be opened. She put it all in my name and so I had to go sign the paperwork.

When making arrangements at the funeral home, Stewart. showed up. When I saw him walk in the funeral home wearing sunglasses, I knew what needed to happen. Stewart. and his family had a habit of making a scene at funerals.

In fact, at my stepdaughter Nicole's funeral, three years earlier, Stewart's mom fell on the floor yelling "my poor baby girl".

There was actually no reason for her to even miss Nicole because she never saw her. She never had anything to do with any of Stewart's children.

So, I walked up to him and politely told him he needed to remove his sunglasses because the sun was not shining in the building. I told him that they would respect my son. I also told him that if either he or any of his family did anything stupid that I would call the police and have them removed. In fact, I knew most of the people on the police force so they would already be at the funeral.

Up until this point, I had always let the people around me make most of the decisions in my life. I never really had any self-confidence or self-worth. I did not think my decisions mattered. I was always made fun of and called names. If you do not make a decision or mistake then you save yourself some heartache, no one can blame you.

This time was different! I was going to plan this funeral, along with his brothers and sisters.

This did not go over very well with those people that had always taken control of my life. I was belittled and talked about. I was still trying to wrap my mind around what was happening to my life and having these battles all along the way.

I was told "shame on me" because I didn't "include" my sister, Cindy, in the funeral. Basically, all you do at a funeral for a family member is sit around and talk to other family members, unless you are the one in the casket. So, I did not even know what she expected me to do about that. She was mad and sat on the back row almost the entire time because she was not included.

I was talking to the funeral director at one point and told him that I was planning to sit with the body all night. (It is a southern thing) My youngest sister, Janet overheard me and asked if I wanted her to stay with me. I said "sure, if you want to". Well, Cindy heard that Janet was staying the night with me and got upset because I did not ask her. It was not intentional or even a thought in my head at this point.

During the funeral services I did not cry much. (I do not like making a scene or drawing attention to myself) It was when I would get home that I would just fall to pieces. Dave would not say anything, he would just hold me tight and let me sob for hours.

The funeral was beautiful and the amount of people that poured into and attended the service was phenomenal. It truly was a great testimony to his short life here on earth.

We buried my son on November 1st, 2006, on all Saint's Day.

After the funeral, I was grieving hard and did not even want to leave my house. I would not go hang out with friends or Dave. I stayed home and painted walls and planted flowers. At one point my 9-year-old, Joseph, told me, "Mom, if you plant anymore flowers, we won't even have any grass to mow."

Dave was continuing to be so supportive for me. He brought me flowers 2 – 3 times a week, just to get a smile out of me. He, cooked for me, drew my bath water, brought me glasses of wine and anything he could think of to get me to be my old self. Dave tried to make me happy again, but I could not even find myself. After a long painstaking year of watching me fall apart and cry all the time, Dave left me. He hated seeing me cry all the time and when we would leave for work to go our separate ways, he would cry too. Now, with my rock gone, I got even sadder. I was not only grieving but now I was depressed. I started drinking even more and more. I did not care about anything. I really do not think that it was so much that I did not care as it was that I did not know how to care anymore. It took every ounce of energy just to exist for my children.

My happiness had been sucked right out from under me and there was absolutely nothing I could do about it. My fight for life was gone.

It was at this time my 16-year-old son Michael, became my rock. He would hold me and hug me and tell me it would be ok. He would even cry with me sometimes. I know it had to be hard for him too because he and Martin. were only 18 months apart. Michael was a lifesaver for me.

Chapter 12

The Medium

The Medium

Michael kept a close eye on me for a while. He always talked about one of his basketball friends named Eli. Michael continued to tell me that I needed to meet Eli's mom, Ella. He kept on and on and finally talked me into coming to one of his basketball games and sitting with Ella and her husband Greg. We had great conversation and she invited me over to their house that next week for a Super Bowl party. She told me to come early so that we could chat. Ella and I got along great and had many laughs. I helped her shop, cook, and set up for the Super Bowl party. We became friends immediately. She has a beautiful soul.

After the Super Bowl Party, Ella would invite me to go on picnics at the park with her family and other outings that they would have. Ella told me a few times about her neighbors, Dana, and Sam. She said that every now and then the neighbors would have a Medium come to their house to give readings. Ella told me I needed to meet the medium.

One day Ella called and said that Greg was at work and when he got off at 6pm he wanted me and Ella to meet him at the casino to eat some King Crab Legs. I agreed to go, and I picked Ella up at her house.

As we were leaving Ella's house she said "Oh, look at all the cars, Donna. They must have the Medium there." Ella told me to pull into Sam and Dana's driveway. I pulled into the driveway and Ella went to the door. When Ella came back to the car, she said they were only having a Tupperware party. We got a good laugh out of that.

About a week later I went to Ella's house again and she gave me a phone number. She told me it was the number for the Medium and that I should call her. I told her that I would and stuck the number in my huge purse.

Several days later I was crossing the bridge on my way home from work. At the foot of the bridge was a wreck. We were going to be stuck in traffic for about 2 hours. I sat for several minutes and then I remembered the number in my purse and thought "Why not?".

I dialed the number of Verniece Wyles. When Verniece answered she said "Hello, I've been expecting your call. Your son is very persistent." Anyone that ever knew my son, knew this to be a very true statement. I knew that Verniece was from Missouri and as I talked to her, I learned she was actually in Sulphur, La at that moment. Verniece and I scheduled a reading for later that night because she was flying back home the following morning.

I called Michael and he told me that he did not believe in Mediums. He had read in the Bible that you were not supposed to talk to dead people. I told him that he did not have to be there, but I was meeting with her. Joseph was near me when I spoke with Michael and decided he did not want to be there either. I told him he could go in his room and that I would meet with her anyway. So, when it was time Joseph went in his room but left the door open so that he could listen.

When I met with Verniece the first thing she told me is that she believes in God and that you should never believe a Medium that denounces God. After a short while, Joseph came out of his room because he was hearing the accuracy of her reading. There are things she told us that no one could know.

You can read below, the actual story posted on Verniece Wyles' Website: (names have been changed in this book)

www.sentinelsvoice.com under subtitle Paranormal stories:

A Mother's Story

I want to share a testimonial from a Mother I did a Reading for in Sulphur, Louisiana in March 2008. Here is her personal experience of that paranormal meeting in Sulphur, Louisiana.

The way I came to meet Verniece Wyles is a story in itself. As my friend, Ella and I were talking about my son who passed away last year, Ella mentioned to me that her neighbors, Dana and Sam, had hosted a Medium, Verniece Wyles, to visit in their home in Sulphur, Louisiana. Verniece conducted a Group Reading for local residents who wanted to attend the group for messages from loved ones. The subject of Verniece came up a couple of times for the next month.

One night as we were leaving Ella's house, Ella told me to pull into her neighbor's driveway, and she would get the name and number for me from them.

So, the next afternoon as I left work, I had a strong feeling to call Verniece right away. When I called her on her cell phone, she was very shocked to learn I was from Sulphur because she said she was just driving right into the middle of Sulphur as we spoke on the cell phone!

I knew she lived in Missouri. I was surprised myself to learn she was here where I live. I asked her for a Reading appointment. Verniece told me she was leaving the next morning for Houston for nine days. She suggested we meet before she left town. We would meet later in the evening.

When Verniece arrived for the Reading, I was of course nervous. I did not know what to expect. The only thing that Verniece knew was that my Son, Martin had died in a car accident. She knew nothing else about me.

She explained that I was a person that needed something to "WOW" me. I am not a very emotional person, so it has to be something big to impress me! She was right about that!

Verniece said that she was hearing that Martin's seat belt broke and he was thrown from the car. She had no way of knowing this!

Then she said that around the time when my Son died a female passenger in the car accident with him survived the wreck. She was in the hospital. This person had a bracelet or something that appeared like a bracelet on her wrist. This bracelet was something that my Son had given this girl because they were close. This person was in the hospital a while after the accident. I told Verniece this was true that his girlfriend survived the crash. I would talk with his girlfriend to find out if he gave her such an item. I would let Verniece know what I found out.

Verniece told me my Son wanted me to know he had so many people he wanted to communicate with after the accident. He stayed by the girl's bedside all the time she was there because he was concerned, she would not make it. Maybe she would not want to live.

He wanted me to tell her he is drawn to the light around others but when she is depressed, he cannot get her to know he is there for her. He wants her to be happy again.

Then Verniece asked me if I worked in an office. I told her that I did. She said that Martin was concerned for my neck and shoulder pain. It was caused by the way I used the phone. Then she said, "No... wait, it's your cell phone." I told her I am always on the cell phone that way. I told her I had been seeing a chiropractor but had not made the connection with the cell phone as the problem.

She said Martin watches over me. He is very proud of me. He told me that he was like in a valley; some place that was a lot like where we went as a family on vacations. He said he was happy and at peace in this place. I could then visualize where Martin must be now. Many of our vacations were in nature with beautiful valleys and water. He knew this would help me feel better having this visual image of him in a peaceful valley. As a family we were together in places like this on our vacations when he was with us.

She also told me he was happy I was planning a vacation. She said be sure and take motion sickness pills! Verniece had no way of knowing this, but I had just signed up for a cruise. And, my younger son has issues with motion sickness.

She told me Martin wanted me to have a health exam as soon as I could. He is concerned about my health. I have been meaning to take time to schedule that routine appointment.

I ask Verniece if Martin had any messages for his siblings. She looked at my youngest son and gave him this message. Martin said: "I used to take you fishing a lot. It isn't your fault that I died." Verniece had no way of knowing that my youngest son had been blaming himself for Martin's passing.

Martin used to take him fishing a lot at our old house that had a pond on the property. Verniece said that Martin wanted my oldest son to take him fishing now that he is no longer with them.

Verniece looked at a family portrait on the living room wall. She said that Martin was telling her my oldest daughter was so bossy, but he really loved her. That was what Martin would have said. Martin had messages for her and my 17-year-old son. I asked her if Martin had messages for my stepdaughter. Verniece said they were very close, and Martin told Kelly very personal things in his life. This is true about what she told me.

Verniece asked me who in the family liked strawberries. I said that Martin did. I used to make him strawberry jelly.

He liked it because it did not have seeds in it. he loved that jelly. I have thought about that a lot since his death.

Verniece asked who had felt Martin's presence at the bedside and I told her that I had. She told me that he sat on my bed at night while I was asleep to be near me. He said if he had known what he knew now, he would have done more of that to talk with me when he was alive. Verniece had no way of knowing this. My kids come in my bedroom and sit on my bed to talk with me.

She had no way of knowing that after Martin's death, on several occasions the touch light table lamp at my bedside went off and on without any reason. this fits what she said about Martin being at my bedside after his death.

Verniece told me that Martin wanted me to know that he arranged this personal Reading in perfect timing. We are convinced now that he did! A lot had to happen to make this possible for me to connect with Martin when I did.

He told me about words to a song that he wanted me to look up on the internet. he wanted me to get the CD and listen to the words. He said this was for the two women he loved. His girlfriend and me. Verniece had heard the tune being sung in her thoughts but did not know the title of the song.

When Verniece stood up to leave, I approached her to hug her. She was obviously surprised about something.

Just as I was about to hug her, she said: "I just heard Martin say, "I want to hug my mother through you!" Martin had not gotten to say goodbye to me when he died in the accident.

About a week after the Reading, I had been looking up the words to the song that Verniece had mentioned in the Reading. Verniece called me because she had a strong urge to call me to know if I was doing okay. I told her I could not find the words she had sung in the phrases of the song at the Reading. She laughed and said: "That is because I realized after the Reading it was two different songs!" One song was for me, and one was for his girlfriend who survived the car wreck. And both songs were totally appropriate for a mother and a girlfriend.

I was able to meet with Martin's girlfriend about a month after the Reading with Verniece. Martin did give her something that was like a bracelet. It was a sweat band that she wears on her wrist. I told her about Martin's visit and his message of encouragement to her. She was so excited. She had a genuine smile on her face. There was a twinkle in her eyes I have not seen since the accident!

She said she would work on not being so depressed now because she wanted to feel Martin's presence around her. I am so excited for her. I wrote the words to the song on paper for her that Martin gave me in the Reading. She sent me a text message on the following Monday saying she heard the actual song on the radio! This is a sign to me that he is with her! Thank you so much, Verniece, for what you have done for us! (Donna Jean, Sulphur, Louisiana March 2008)

A couple months later I had another story post on Ms. Wyle's site

Searching for a Lost Cat

I received an e-mail from a female client out of state that was searching for her cat. She told me if I had any message that would help find her cat, please let her know. The cat is an indoor cat and accidently escaped out the door. The woman was very concerned for the cat's safety. She was hoping she would find her cat real soon.

When I read the e-mail, the immediate message I received from Spirit was this: "Tell her to look around the trash can."

When I checked back with the client through e-mail, I told her what I had heard from Spirit. I asked her to explain what she thought Spirit meant by the message I received.

She was so happy when she e-mailed me later. She said that she found her cat, very scared but safe. The cat was underneath the deck of the house. The explanation about looking around the trash can was that this woman has a metal trash can on the deck on the back of the house. It is used as a storage container for the dog food. The cat was under the deck!

Nothing is too small a task for Spirit. Everyone and everything matter when it comes to protecting and nurturing life. And that means all life forms here on earth. We are loved and so are the pets in our family. (Verniece, May 2008)

Dave always called to check on me after he left and of course, I was so excited to tell him about the Medium. After the accident there was a nightly occurrence that would happen. I have a touch lamp on the side of my bed that I had gotten from my grandmother and I have had it for many years. After Martin died the light would cycle through low, medium, high then off several times in a row. It did this every night around 10:15pm for months. It was so regular that if it happened and I was brushing my teeth or not in the room, Dave would yell "Hey Donna, Martin is here".

This lamp had never done this before the accident and does not do it anymore. Another thing that would happen was that I would feel cold on the left side of my body if I were laying on my bed. It was cold but comforting. This was all reassurance that my baby boy was still here with his momma.

Chapter 13

Toxic is familiar

Toxic is familiar

Approximately a year had passed since Dave had left and now, he was dating someone else. Some friends of mine introduced me to a guy, George, who they saw around town and thought was a nice guy. He owned his own business in town and seemed to have himself together. He was a load of fun and liked to show off. We eventually started dating.

He had a motor home and we went camping a lot. He had a motorcycle and we went to motorcycle rallies. He had a pontoon boat and a party boat. We were constantly doing things. It was a lot of work getting everything clean and ready before and after trips. It was fun so I participated as much as possible. We went to Key West several times and Cozumel too. Sometimes it was the best time ever but, if he was in a cross mood, it could feel like the worst time of your life. It all depended on his mood. You never knew which one it would be until it hit. If he was in a cross mood, then everything became my fault. He would make sure I was miserable. He was very jealous and always wanted his way. If we were with other people and he was in a cross mood, he would be nice to them and ignore me and act like I had an issue. If we were alone, he would yell and scream. If he was in a good mood, then everything was great, and everyone had a great time. Also, if I was too nice to anyone, he found something wrong with it or if I did not talk to someone, he found something wrong with that too.

One night I was determined to make it a good night. We went to the local bar, as usual, and instead of talking to our normal guy group, I struck up a conversation with the only other girl at the bar. I said hi and bye to our normal friends but kept my distance from the guys.

On the way home George started yelling at me. I said, "What is wrong with you?" He said, "What are you a lesbian, now?" I was so angry with him. When we got back to his house, I threw my things in my car, deleted my number from his phone and went home. He eventually got my number and called me back. I stayed in this twisted relationship for 5 years. I simply did not care enough about myself to make a change. Not to make mention I had grown to love his children and grandchildren. We also had some really great friends. I started keeping track after a couple of years and it was every 30 days when his mood got twisted and he wanted to fight. If he took diet pills that would trigger it too. One time he took me to Key West and stayed on the phone almost the entire trip. Nothing like going on vacation by yourself.

It was a known fact, in his family, that he had these mood swings. If we invited his daughter and son-in-law over for a barbeque, his daughter would call before they showed up and ask, "How is his mood?"

We were at a bike rally once and George's son had come with us. For some stupid reason George got upset and yelled at me, then left the motor home, and slammed the door. His son looked at me and said, "Why do you put up with that?" I told him I do not know and that one day I will get tired of it and walk away.

We had been together for 5 years. He decided he wanted to have Thanksgiving at his house and invite my Mom and Pop. It turned out great. The food was good, and we all enjoyed ourselves. His kids came and my kids came along with my parents. After everyone left and I got everything cleaned up, we made a plan. He said early the next morning he was going to take me to New Orleans to see the Christmas lights because he knew how much I loved Christmas lights. He said we would stop at a couple RV dealers on the way and check out some motorhomes.

So, bright and early the next morning, 5am, we loaded our suitcases and set out for New Orleans. We stopped at every RV dealer from Lake Charles to New Orleans. Finally, we arrive in New Orleans at dark, after RV shopping for hours and hours. He started complaining when we had to pay to park. We walked around the French Quarter and had a couple beers. We did not see any Christmas lights. We went into a local business and inquired about Christmas lights and were told that the lights were down the road at the park just over the bridge from where we were.

It was about a 2 to 4-minute drive. George said "Oh well, we tried"

He stated that he wanted to go to the Casino. I told him that we have Casinos at home and the whole reason for the trip was to see the lights. Then he said he was hungry, so we went to grab a bite to eat. He never mentioned the lights again and neither did I. He continued to walk in front of me the rest of the evening, like I was not with him. At around 9:30 he decides it is time to go. We got in the truck and proceeded to look for a hotel room. He gets us lost several times and we finally find a hotel room out of town at around midnight. We took turns showering and getting ready for bed. While I showered, he was watching TV and I was totally exhausted. When I was done showering, I crawled in the bed and fell asleep. After a few minutes, he woke me up and told me that if we were not going to have sex then he would prefer if I just go sleep in the other bed. I told him it did not matter to me, but that sex would probably be better after I had gotten some rest. George turned off the TV and I dozed off to sleep, again. All of a sudden, I hear a loud bang. I turn on the light and George gets up to pick up the tv remote. He had thrown it against the wall.

I got up and went to the other bed it was now about 2am.

At 7am George gets up and gets dressed. He goes to the hotel lobby and gets himself some coffee while I get dressed. When he returns, he starts the truck and loads his suitcase. I am still getting dressed. He sits in his truck and waits for me to finish getting dressed. George wanted to be sure I knew he was mad and ready to go. I hurry and finish getting dressed, load my suitcase in the truck and we head home. Not many words were said for the first hour on the way home. Did I mention that George likes to argue? I mean, REALLY likes to argue.

He started fussing at me for about 20 minutes. I ask him if he was done and he said yes. So, I started fussing at him and he immediately stopped me. I said" Wait a minute. You said you were done and now it is my turn. So, keep your mouth shut until I'm done and then you can speak." I finished my spill and he did not have anything to say for about 30 minutes, that is when he started again. When he was done, I started. I told him "no worries, when we get back to your house, I will get all my stuff and you will never hear from me again". It was not a pleasant 3-hour drive back to Sulphur.

When we arrived at George's house, I went inside and got all my things. On my way out the door, George said, "You know Donna, we can be friends" I said, "No we can't" and I left.

After I had been back at my house a while, I remembered that I had left my Pampered Chef Pie Stone at his house. I had to call him the next day and go pick it up.

Chapter 14

No Time to Heal

No Time to Heal

After I was done with this last toxic relationship, I decided that it was time to find myself. At this point, I did not even know who I was or what I wanted out of life. I had spent so many years pleasing others that now I was so lost. As I began this journey and started reading self-help books, my youngest son began to rebel. He started when his brother had died but was getting progressively worse. He did not care about school. He did not care if he got in trouble or not. Joseph was only 9 years old when Martin died. Joseph started self-medicating on mild drugs and then when they would not numb his pain, he would try something more powerful.

He would sneak out at night; and do everything I asked him not to do. I remember one day I was at a friend's house visiting, and another one of my friends, Tom, (He worked for the Sheriff's office) asked me "Donna, why is your house being watched by the sheriff's department?" I said "What?" I had no idea what he was talking about. So, about a day or two later I asked my son, Joseph. "Why is the Sheriff's department watching our house?" Joseph became extremely nervous and said, "who told you that?" I told him it did not matter. I asked him "Don't you know, I have friends that are police officers?" My friends all know me well enough to know that I would not do anything illegal. The next day Joseph left my house and was gone for about a month. I did not know where he was or what he was doing until I received a phone call at midnight one night. Joseph was on the phone and asked me to come pick him up.

I showed up to pick Joseph up, on the wrong side of town, When Joseph came out of the house, he looked like a walking skeleton. He was so skinny, and his ankles looked about the size of my wrist.

I later found out that he had been doing Meth. He had not eaten hardly anything since he left my house. The only reason that he had come home was because the drug dealer he was working for had slapped him and told him to go home, He told Joseph that he did not belong there.

I fought Joseph and his drug and attitude problem for a long time. We tried every kind of therapy and counseling I could find. I would get him all straightened out and then he would disappear again. He would break into my house when I was at work. I found out that he would lie to people and tell them I had kicked him out so that they would feel sorry for him and give him money. He would show up, out of the blue, and claim that he was wanting to do better. I would help him out and give him food and a place to stay. I would get him a job. He would work long enough to get a couple of paychecks and then quit and be gone again.

We tried to let him live with his father, who was out of jail now. This is where Joseph. claimed he wanted to be. This, however, did not work out either because he would get into arguments with his stepmom and grandmother while his father was at work. Eventually he came back to live with me.

Again, he was always in trouble at home and at school. I took him to more therapy and counseling. Nothing ever seemed to help. So, before he turned 18, I had his doctor commit him to a rehab clinic. I had a friend that worked for the facility and got him a bed there. He refused to go but the doctor gave him no choice. I had Joseph's father meet me at the doctor's office and we drove him to the facility in Lafayette, Joseph begged for us not to take him and not to commit him. When that would not work, he cursed me and his father for the whole hour drive. It was the most nerve-racking trip I have ever made. We dropped him off and filled out all the paperwork to have him committed. He was there for several months and I would go visit when allowed. We had counseling with the rehab clinic also. Still, nothing seemed to be getting through to him.

Once he had been home, about a month, he went right back to the streets. One time he called me at about 10pm and told me that people were looking for him. He said that they might come hurt me to get to him. He begged me to go stay at a hotel for the night. He told me I would not be safe at home. I did stay in a hotel that night. After this, I bought a gun. I slept lightly for months on end with a gun under my pillow. He has been in and out of jail numerous times. He was sentenced to jail for a year at one point. I would go visit every Saturday. I would keep money on his account so that he could call me. I would even put money on his books so that he could get extras. (Such as soap, toothpaste, toothbrush, and snacks) One Saturday I went to visit, and they tell me that someone had gotten him out of jail. Apparently, Marshall had come to get him out of jail, and no one had even bother to tell me.

It was at this point that I felt so used and mistreated. Now the only help I give him is, I pray for him every morning and every night. The last time he took off with all his things, I told him not to come back. I was so worn out I could not even think straight.

He has been in jail several times since then but does nothing to change the situation. At one point he told me he liked living on the street.

Chapter 15

Starting Over

Starting Over

One day I was sitting at home and the Lord literally spoke to me and said that I needed to move to Arkansas.

I was at a point that I hated my job. I hated my life and the people that surrounded me could not care less about me. Arkansas was a place that I had visited every several months for the last 13 years. My best friend, Marie had moved there with her family after leaving California. I loved going up there and visiting her. Every time I would visit, Marie would tell me I needed to move. I would always tell her that I would not. Sometimes she would even take me to look at houses in her neighborhood that were for sale. So, when the Lord put it on my heart, I did not know what to make of it. I thought maybe it was because I was so unhappy with my life. I prayed on it and the more I prayed the clearer it became. Yes, this is what God wanted me to do. I sat down and wrote Marie a letter and told her what I was planning. When Marie got my letter, she called me crying. She was so excited. I began packing my house room by room. I piled all the boxes in my spare room and put my house on the market. Everything fell into place rather quickly. I sold my house and moved all my belongings into a storage building in Greenbrier, Arkansas. I then moved into the upstairs room at mom's house. I looked for a job in Arkansas, while working in Sulphur, La. I was not having much luck. Marie told me to come move in with her and Karl, I could have the upstairs bedroom and bathroom until I found a job and bought a house. So, that is what I did.

After several months and still no job, I had some doubts. I kept telling myself that God would not have put it on my heart to move and then just let me fail. I kept praying and trusting.

I got in touch with a temp agency and told them I would take anything until the right job came along. They put me to work in the cafeteria at a school. When I tell you this is hard work, it is definitely hard work,

After several weeks of cooking and washing huge pots and pans, I got an interview. I went to a the only 3 story building in downtown Conway for my interview. I met with a gentleman named Todd. He was very polite and was a retired military veteran.

When Todd interviewed me, he said that my resume had everything he was looking for. Todd also told me that it was so strange because his mom's name was Donna too. I was the first interview that day and he told me I was hired! I could start on Monday!

Now, I had my job, that I really liked. I had found a house that was gorgeous, and I did not think I could afford, but I did. It was all just a smooth process. After 2 years at my job and in my house things were perfect. My boss and his family are an extension of my family!! He is like a brother to me.

For five years, I had been trying to get mentally healthy. I had not dated. I was just trying to heal my heart and my mind. I read lots of self-help books and just hung out with my friends.

Marie told me that there was a guy that comes in the bank where she works, and he was single. She had known him for a while and that he had been divorced for about 2 years. She had been telling me this since I moved here. I thought she was telling me this because she did not want me to move back to Louisiana. But on August 7th, 2018 she called and told me she had given this guy my phone number. Sure enough, that evening a guy, James called me for a date. James told me to figure out where I wanted to go and when and let him know. So, the next day, I called him back and told him we could go Thursday night to dinner.

I had been single for 5 years and had not even thought about dating. I was so nervous for this date. I felt like a schoolgirl again.

I normally would not allow a stranger to come pick me up at my house, but my friend had known him for several years. So, I let him come pick me up. He was 20 minutes late for our first date. He apologized and said that he would work on that. He told me he was always late. We went to a local restaurant and had great conversation, with no awkward silent moments. We sat at the restaurant and talked for hours. We did not even realize that it had rained until we were leaving. As we left the restaurant, he opened the door for me to get into his car. I looked up and there was just one little opening in the cloud, and you could see all the stars. I pointed that out to him, and he looked up also. After he looked up at the stars he leaned over and kissed me. It was so perfect.

He had the prettiest blue eyes; was handsome, and he worked out and he was very interested in me!! Wow!!

We began seeing each other a lot. He called me beautiful all the time, even when I was not wearing makeup and my hair was a mess. We had lots of laughs and enjoyed each other's company. We decided that one weekend we would go spend the weekend in Branson, Missouri and check out the Christmas lights. James's mom owned a time share and we would stay in a condo there. We had been dating a little over 3 months and things were going well.

On the way to Branson, James was holding my hand. Out of nowhere he said "You know I don't want a serious relationship. I've only been divorced for 2 years" I was going to let go of his hand and he grabbed it back and said "but, I don't want to see anyone else, just you. I just do not want a serious relationship. I thought back to when I was dating Dave for 5 years and would not let him say he loved me. I had been hurt too many times,

So, I said" No problem, you will figure it out." I could see where he was coming from.

We had a great time in Branson. We saw the Christmas lights, rode the new Time Traveler rollercoaster, saw some shows, and watched the Christmas parade. I felt like a 53-year-old kid. It was terrific. After we returned home, he was at my house almost every day. He came with me to a wedding in Louisiana and we stayed at mom's house. He volunteered to come with me to pick up and drop off my grandkids. He came to my boss' house for Thanksgiving and I went to his Mom's house. Then for Christmas, I went shopping with him and helped him pick out all the presents for his friends and family. When Christmas time came, I went with him to his work luncheon. Then he invited me to his Aunt's house to open presents. We went to his Mom's house to open presents. It was a great couple of days. When we returned to my house, I tried to give him his Christmas presents, and he would not take them. He said he had not gotten me anything. I was totally blown away. We had spent months talking about Christmas and would say random things and say "That is what I'm getting you for Christmas"

So, I put his presents in the spare bedroom and they were never mentioned again. I eventually brought them back to the store. He still does not know what they were.

We continued to date and hang out. We would go eat, listen to bands, and play pool.

In February, for Valentine's Day, he showed up at my office with a dozen roses, a coffee mug with hearts on it and a little stuffed teddy bear. That was an awesome surprise!! It really surprised me after the whole "Christmas thing"

About six months into dating we were laying in the bed one morning and he said, "You know with all my wives I proposed after 6 months?" I really did not know what to say and so I just said, "Oh really?" That was all that was said. I am still not sure why he even mentioned that.

A short time after this he started creating distance between us. The only times we would go on dates is when his friend Daniel was with us. We still had fun and laughed just as much as before. He just was not coming over as much. Although he started inviting me to go to the gym with him. I would go because I love that kind of stuff. Then we would go back to my house to eat supper or go to a restaurant.

One Friday night it was storming like crazy and James came over. We were trying to figure out what we wanted to do. He fell asleep on the couch. So, I let him sleep, while I watched tv. I woke him up when it was time to go to bed. The next morning, we had coffee and then he left. It turned out to be a gorgeous day. I sent James a text that afternoon and said, "Hey since it isn't storming tonight, let's go play pool later." He texted me back and said he was planning to go watch a basketball game for his cousin's child but maybe after that. I said ok and for him to just let me know. I did not hear from James so about 10:30 I get ready and go to bed. At 11pm he texts me and said "Ok, I'm here come meet me". I was so mad. He had plenty of time to let me know he was on his way

(He lived 30 minutes away). He could have come picked me up. He was only about 7 minutes away from my house. I was extremely mad so, I texted "The End" He texted me back and said, "Do What?"   sure, he figured it out and he did not text back. He did not come to my house to see what made me mad. Nothing! Later that next week, he texted several times and I never answered. After a couple of weeks, he texted me a very lengthy text and said he wanted to talk to me. So, I agreed, and we did.

James apologized and said he just does not know what he wants. He told me he was sorry because he knew he was a jerk to me.

I told him about all the things he did to hurt me, and he agreed that he was a jerk. He told me he never wanted to hurt me again. He said if I ever needed anything to let him know and he would be glad to help me. He did come to my house once after that to fix my lawn mower and even finished mowing my grass one Sunday. My friend Dana saw him at church and told him I was having problems getting my mower started so he called me and came over to help. James continued to text me "Hello beautiful, have a great day. Big hugs and kisses" with lots of kissy emojis behind the message.

He did come visit me at the gym a few times and just sat and talked with me.

Then he started dating someone else (I heard it was two months before we were done, which would explain a lot, but I cannot be sure)

He continued to text me until he and the new girlfriend went on vacation with their families and they posted a picture on Facebook.

Dating James, I did meet a great group of girls that would go listen to bands. I have made some lifelong friends with them and I am thankful for that.

It makes me angry that while James was dating this girl, he continued to string me along and text me daily.

I have decided that at 53 years old, it is probably best for me to just be happy and forget about all the other stuff.

I now hang out with several groups of friends. We go to dances, we rent houses and cabins every year. We kayak, shop, go to concerts, play card games, drink, build bonfires and just enjoy life.

I have no idea what God has in store for me, but I will continue to enjoy life with my friends, kids, and grandkids.

I will not give up on a happy life and I am not done living yet!!

To God Be the Glory
Philippians 4:20

About the Author

Donna Jean grew up with lots of abuse, drama, and disappointment. Through lots of her life she was just on survival mode. She raised her children and just struggled through it. We always go back to the familiar, so in her marriages it was always, abuse, drama, and disappointment. Finally, after losing her son in 2006 she decided she would start a new path to healing herself. It took 13 years with lots of back sliding, research, and prayers. Finally, Donna has come to a happy place in her life where she knows who she is, what she wants and not "settling for mediocre" any longer.

Through her ups and downs she has always believed in God and a better life.

She is now living her best life and exploring all that God and this great planet have to offer. We all have our own journey to go through in this life but,

Donna decided to share her struggles in hopes that perhaps it would help someone else. She hopes and prays for each one of you that reads her book that you also will find your way on your journey to live a better life.

YOU DESERVE IT!!

Made in the USA
Middletown, DE
19 July 2020